Frank Frog Feels Foolish.

(in the 'Alphabet Animals of Australia series')

Written by

MAUREEN LARTER

Illustrated by Patsy Seager

©2017.

Copyright © 2017 by Maureen Larter.

First published 2017 by Sweetfields Publishing

956 Comboyne Rd, Cedar Party, NSW Australia 2429

email: maureenlarter@gmail.com

twitter: @maureenlarter

blog:- www.readeatdream.net

ISBN:- 978-0-9876393-2-5

A catalogue record for this book is available from

The National Library of Australia, Canberra, ACT, Australia.

Set in Mongolian Baiti font by Maureen Larter, Cedar Party, NSW, Australia.

Illustrations © 2017 by Patsy Seager

Children's picture book in the series 'Alphabet Animal of Australia.

About the Author

Maureen Larter was born in England in the late 1940's and came over to Australia when still a toddler. She is a teacher of piano and violin, and lives on the lower Mid North Coast of New South Wales, Australia.

She lives on a small-holding of 12 acres, and does her best to live self-sufficiently, while taking care of the soil and the environment. In the past, she has taught English, Social Studies, Music and Mathematics in High Schools within Australia, as well as living in China for a short time, teaching English. She has also taught in Cambodia.

On wet days, when she can't be out in her garden, and there are no students commandeering her time, she loves to sit and write. She writes children's stories and short stories, as well as occasional articles for magazines.

She has recently (under the pen-name Marguerite Wellbourne) branched out into adult drama.

About the Illustrator.

Patsy Seager was born south of Sydney, Australia in the early 1950s. She was raised on a property that grew fruit commercially.

After school, she worked as a jillaroo on sheep and cattle properties. Another job later on was as a nursing aide and then she eventually became a sterilizing technician.

Throughout her life, she enjoyed drawing, but due to family commitments, this fell by the wayside.

She ran two riding clubs for local children, teaching them the basics of riding and looking after their horses and the equipment. Her other work included looking after birds as a volunteer for a rescue association.

Only now has she had the opportunity and time to illustrate children's books, one of the dreams she has had all her life.

Other books she has illustrated are:-

'Candy Cow and the Caterpillar' written by Maureen Larter.

'Frank Frog Feels Foolish' written by Maureen Larter.

She is currently working on:-

'Peter Platypus's Pond' written by Maureen Larter.

'Bartholomew' written by Elizabeth Kempers.

OTHER BOOKS BY MAUREEN LARTER

1. **Good Health** – The Soil
2. Yearly guide to planting flowers and vegetables

Gardening Guides
1. Summer
2. Autumn
3. Winter
4. Spring

Adult Drama
(under the pen-name Marguerite Wellbourne)

Tarnished Gems
Ordeal by Innocence

Business (How to) Booklet

The Start of Something Big

Short Stories

1. Book 1 - At the Beach - (4 stories)
2. Book 2 – Predicaments – (5 stories)

Books for Middle school

Fairies from Aurora Village Series
1. Broken Wing.
2. Spiders, Lizards and Flies
3. Cave of the Golden Bower Bird

Petey - Missing the Migration
In Search of the Elusive Panda - A Kathy Edwards Adventure

For Toddlers

What about me?
Arabella's Tree

Alphabet Animals of Australia Series

1. Angus Ant and the Acrobats
2. Betty Bee's Birthday Bash
3. Ben Brolga's Band
4. Candy Cow and the Caterpillar
5. Cassie Crocodile Catches a Cold
6. Dorothy Dog and the Dangerous Dragonfly.
7. Evie Emu's Encounter
8. Frank Frog Feels Foolish
9. Giddy the Galah
10. Helen Heron and the Helicopter
11. Iggy Ibis is Important
12. John Jabiru and the Jolly Jam tin
13. Kathy Koala's Kerfuffle

This is an ongoing series. There are many more to come.

Frank Frog sat on a lily pad in his favourite waterhole.

The sounds of the bush were all around him. Cicadas were chirping. Rainbow lorikeets were chattering and the Noisy Mynahs were having an argument in the Eucalypt tree.

It didn't worry Frank at all.

A reed growing

next to him

shaded him from

the afternoon sun

and kept

him cool.

He was day-dreaming.

Several tadpoles swam up to the surface of the pond and stared at him.

But Frank didn't answer and the tadpoles swam away.

By this time, Frank was imagining a beautiful castle. It had flags on the towers, and curtains at the windows.

Frank sighed with pleasure.

Near Frank's head buzzed a fly.

A mosquito hummed and a bee droned.

A dragonfly whirred.

Even an ant sat and stared.

Frank just smiled

Several other friends came and looked at Frank, too. There were some ladybirds and flying ants.

There were some bush flies and two fairy wrens, too.

The flies muttered to each other.

"What is wrong with that frog?" said one.

"He hasn't got his eyes open. That's strange!" said the small one.

"He does look silly, sitting on that leaf, just smiling to himself, doesn't he?" agreed another.

While everyone was crowded around looking at Frank, an amazing thing happened. Frank moved his lips, closed his eyes even tighter ... and ...

gave the air a very loud kiss!

All the animals around the waterhole stopped what they were doing and looked at Frank with astonishment.

Whatever was Frank doing?

Two Willy Wagtails flew down to look.

The kookaburras began to laugh and the Echidna snorted noisily.

A couple of Noisy Mynahs squabbled about the frog's funny face and a Koala in the closest tree boomed out very loudly.

They all thought it was rather amusing.

Now ... Frank frog had no idea that he was being watched. He was having a lovely dream.

He could see his favourite frog, and he blew up his voice sac, made a loud croak and gave her a huge kiss.

In fact, he croaked so loudly he woke himself up.

He looked around.

He was surprised to see all the animals staring at him.

He quickly jumped off the lily pad and disappeared under the water.

Underneath the water, all the tadpoles were swimming around looking at him.

Frank felt really foolish.

One brave little tadpole swam up to Frank.

That was when Frank decided to tell them the truth.

He called a meeting and jumped back onto his lily pad.

Everyone was silent
and the tadpoles
came to the surface.

Everyone listened.

Frank cleared his throat.

In a very loud voice he spoke.

Everyone clapped and cheered.

Frank didn't feel foolish anymore.

Projects for schools.

1. See if you can find some tadpoles in a local waterway and catch a few. Look after them and watch them turn into frogs.

2. Do a study on healthy ponds. If you can get permission, construct a pond at your school.

3. Do a project on all the different types of frogs and toads.

4. Write a story about one of your night dreams. Do dreams have meanings? Research this possibility.

5. Discuss the dreams and ambitions of everyone in the class. Are your dreams a possibilty?

6. Have a discussion of ways the world could become a better and more peaceful planet. Why are there wars?

7. Have a fund-raising day and give the money raised to a Landcare project to save our waterways.

Written by Maureen Larter

Illustrated by Patsy Seager

©2017

www.ingramcontent.com/pod-product-compliance
Lightning Source LLC
Chambersburg PA
CBHW041749290426

44112CB00004B/56